Lessons
from the
Mahaw
Bog

Lessons
from the
Mahaw
Bog

JEAN DICKERSON

ARPress
ILLUMINATING IDEAS.
EMPOWERING VOICES

ARPress
45 Dan Road Suite 5
Canton MA 02021

Hotline: 1(888) 821-0229
Fax: 1(508) 545-7580

Ordering Information:
Quantity sales. Special discounts are available on quantity purchases by corporations, associations, and others. For details, contact the publisher at the address above.

Printed in the United States of America.

ISBN-13:	Paperback	979-8-89389-735-7
	eBook	979-8-89389-736-4

Library of Congress Control Number: 2024922138

Table of Contents

Acknowledgements...vii
Dedication ix
Prologue...xi

Young Girl 1

Teenage Girl-Young Adult 5

Challenges of Getting 6

Young Teacher and College Years 18

Marriage and Family...29

Mid Teaching Years...32

Later Teaching Years-Retirement.............................37

Reflection..39
Epilogue..47

Acknowledgements

Navigators often consult their compasses to determine their direction. A teacher is like a compass; they keep students on their learning course. Teachers consult their professional compasses to help students learn.

The story of this teacher whose character, strength and perseverance always shone through.

Because this teacher was our mother, my sister and I had to share her with hundreds of students on school days. Away from school she insisted on our growing up with well-rounded experiences, piano lessons, recitals, shopping, visiting relatives, chores, gardening, homework, travel, and play.

I dedicate this book to my sons, nieces and nephew who have made extraordinary accomplishments.

Special dedications to Devon, Jared, Jr., Jayden, Jaycen, Kobe and Kade who are pursuing great opportunities.

Dedication

This book is dedicated to all the courageous women of the world.

Prologue

A compelling personal story of one Black Teacher of the early 20th century.

This is the personal story of one Black teacher during segregated America, but it is a true representation of the events, issues, experiences, and outcomes of thousands of educators during that era.

Black Educators in segregated society were in a class by themselves. This story exposes how Black teachers aided African American Education and played a pivotal role in the education of Blacks during segregation. They taught, created a caring climate, and advocated for the needs of their students as is evident in this story.

This story exposes a period in United States history that should be known and remembered.

Young Girl

1918-1923

Annie woke up, looked out her window to see rain. She hoped this would be a light rain and would not be enough to swell the creek. If the creek rose too high, she could not cross, which meant that she could not get to school on time or not at all. Sometimes Mrs. Belton, the teacher, could not get to school on time depending on the amount of rain, because she had to cross Ferguson Creek to get to the quarters, in town where the school was located. All children and the teacher walked to school. School could be closed for days in the winter, depending on the weather. She and Julia Owens were finishing up a report in Social Studies to be presented on Friday. Annie never liked to miss school but knew that the weather sometimes closed school. The school was held in the small unpainted wooden structure and when it rained hard it was so loud hitting the tin roof until Mrs. Belton would have the students lay their heads down on the table until the class could hear again. Some students had to be awakened when the rained lessened so that all could hear the teacher.

Annie was now in 6th grade. Since she started school, she got up at five o'clock A.M. to take care of her morning chores. Rain or shine, she fed the chickens, gathered the eggs, and opened the gate to the chicken yard so they could roam during the day. She carefully placed the eggs in a basket lined with straw. She took the eggs inside and placed them on salt in the large ceramic vase that sat on the floor by the old icebox on the opposite side of the kitchen from the stove. *The vase was a special piece purchased by her mother in 1900 at the hardware store in Pleasant Hill and has been handed down for three generations.*

1

When Annie returned to the house and put the eggs away, she put on her school clothes, gathered her books, and sat down at the table for breakfast. Her mother got up early and prepared breakfast on the huge wood stove. From the smells in the kitchen, Annie knew what she would eat for breakfast: pork sausage, thick crispy slab bacon, grits, oatmeal, milk and cornbread, hoe cakes or biscuits with preserves, pure cane molasses or sorghum. She never went to school without breakfast and learned later in life as a teacher and mother that it was an important meal to get the day started.

There were no hot lunches in the schools in rural Louisiana in the 1920's. Some children went without food all day. Annie took lunch in an empty syrup tin bucket. Food in the bucket on a given day included biscuits, hoe cakes, thick slab bacon, sausage, and molasses. Leftovers from dinner were also placed in the tin lunch bucket; cornbread, greens, baked sweet potato or cracklings. Sometimes a piece of in season fruit was plucked from one of the many fruit trees on the family farm to put in lunch can. There was no stove or lunchroom at the old school building.

Time to start the four mile walk to school. There were no children in the houses during the first mile. In the house just before the creek lived the three Davis children. Octavia was third grade, Bessie and Dessie were in first grade. They could see Annie in the distance as they waited for her to get to their front yard.

Annie usually helped the twins with carrying an item so they could all walk faster.

The light rain that fell was not enough to swell the creek. Once they crossed the creek, they came to the red clay dirt road. This road was dusty when dry and soggy and muddy, boggy, and harsh when wet. All who lived out in the country knew that it was the only way to get to the main road to go into town. They walked about a mile on the clay road, then to Grady's store at the corner of the main road into town, another two miles. After about two miles the quarters came into sight. They knew they could go through the west side of the quarters to reach the school on the east side. By this time on the route there were more children at different places along the road; some early some late.

Annie thought "thank goodness," that it was a light rain and school would not be interrupted.

When they arrived at the school on a rainy day, they put their lunch buckets in the corner, hung their coats on their chairs, took seats at their table and waited for the teacher to give instructions. On a clear day, they could play outside until Mrs. Belton rang the bell. Students lined up in front of the door, boys in one line and girls in another.

* * * * *

There were about twelve students in the school with one teacher. Grade levels were grouped as 1-3, 4-6, 7, 8. The older children helped the younger ones. Annie was often put in charge of the class when the teacher stepped outside. Books were hand–me-downs from the white school. They were used year after year and were torn, missing pages and written in. Mrs. Belton called out grade and subject groups to teach all during the day. Students who were not in the teaching group worked at their desks.

Art and music were taught with the full group. Art activities included coloring with crayons, tracing items from nature, holiday pictures, leaves, rocks, flowers, folding paper patterns and tracing patterns from books. Mrs. Belton bought crayons and paper for art activities. Music was singing, clapping songs. No dancing was allowed. Songs from church were performed in school. There were no instruments. Some students in 7th and 8th grades had good singing voices. Alma Jemison led songs in the church choir; she mostly led the singing during music class.

Music and art were held one day a week, extra study one day and play two days outdoors. There was a thirty-minute recess at ten o'clock every day. The procedure to leave the class was the same every day and each time the class transitioned. Mrs. Belton said "stand, turn, pass." She called out each command and waited until every student had completed that one, then she called the next. Students did not play around or "goof off."

At the end of the school day, Annie felt good about the report she and Julia were working on.

The routine at the end of day was like the morning. Students gathered their belongings and waited to be dismissed. Mrs. Belton called out what the assignments were as reminders. Students were dismissed in groups depending on which direction they walked home.

She called Annie's name, Ferguson Creek and the names of the children walking with her.

On the walk home there were more people stirring, working in their gardens, washing, or just sitting on porches. They spoke and sent messages to parents of the children. Miss Petsie always asked about or sent a message to her mother; pears will be ripe soon, watermelons are ready. During winter season, most people were inside huddled around their wood stoves and fireplaces keeping warm.

Once home, Annie changed clothes and tended to her afternoon chores. She gathered the eggs, swept the chicken yard, scattered feed, and went to corral the chickens back to the yard. When most were back inside the fence, she closed the gate and called "here chickey" for the strays. She opened the gate for each one as they straggled in. All chickens had to be accounted for. She knew each one and exactly which was missing. Having to practice this accountability for these living creatures formed a pattern for Annie as she took on the responsibility of her students, years later, in her teaching career. Annie's outdoor chores were finished. Once back inside she helped her mother and older sister cook dinner and clean the kitchen. After dinner she did schoolwork and read.

Teenage Girl-Young Adult

1926-1937

Annie was now in 8th grade, her last year at the Elizabeth Church School. Up to this point all of her education had been in this one building on the church campus. In the south, many elementary schools for blacks were often located on church campuses. The church provided the land for the school. This formed "a community" which consisted of church, school, and neighborhood. Members of the community supported the teacher and the school. Elizabeth School had supporters who did construction on building, cleaned the grounds, cut wood for the heater in winter. The teacher, Mrs. Belton, was very much appreciated for her work. The ladies baked desserts for holidays. The men brought game and fish from hunting and fishing.

Annie Williams 1929, Age 16

Challenges of Getting

A High School Education

There was not a high school for blacks in the town of Pleasant Hill. Blacks who wanted to pursue a high school education had to go to Many, Louisiana, Sabine Parish, located 20 miles away and room with families. The other option was to go to Mansfield, Louisiana, DeSoto Parish, the neighboring parish to the north about 25 miles, rent rooms in homes or stay at a boarding house.

This was devastating for so many and a critical point during this time in history when opportunities were lost for so many black students. Most families could not afford to send their children out of town to get a high school education. Students in these families ended their education and took jobs working in the fields, in kitchens, day work and whatever they could find. Work was back breaking with very little pay.

Many families became part of the migration out of the south for better opportunities for their children and to get decent pay for the work they did. So, they left Pleasant Hill to go to cities in the west, east and large cities in the south.

Annie's mother knew they had no relatives in either place and did not want her to go, so young, where there were no relatives and rooming with strangers.

Annie's mother was born in 1871 and completed eighth grade around 1885 in a church school her father, helped to start. Leaving home to go to high school was not even an option for her in the late 1800's.

Annie's mother had a niece in Pineland, Texas, who had left a few years earlier for her children to attend high school. This niece had a daughter the same age as Annie. She welcomed Annie to come and live in the boarding home that she and her husband lived in and ran for students to come to complete high school. During the summer prior to leaving for Pineland, Annie worked the garden, picked vegetables and fruits, helped to gather crops, and helped to sew some of the clothes she would take with her.

Parents had asked her to teach their children during the summer. Annie knew that the Mahaw Bogs were dry in summer and would be a natural cover from the hot sun. She chose a cool, shady spot out under the edge of the bogs, to teach the children. She helped some of the younger children that lived in the quarters with reading, writing, spelling and arithmetic. She noticed that teaching under the bogs in summer, the children were relaxed and retained what they had learned. The mothers gave her pieces of cloth, handkerchiefs, and scarves as gifts. Mothers even gave her jars of mahaw jelly which was freshly canned in spring.

Mahaw is a wild berry that grows on trees in Louisiana and other southern states. Mahaw trees grow in moist creek bottoms under large hardwood trees. The fruit ripens in April-May. The mahaw swamp was adjacent to the creek Annie crossed to walk to school.

Annie, her sister, brother and other family members had always gone into the mahaw swamps to gather the berries to make jelly. The jelly was a beautiful crimson color and was delicious with her mother's hot buttermilk biscuits and a piece of thick crispy fried bacon, with the skin on.

That summer passed quickly with all the many things to do to prepare for family survival during the winter and her going off to high school. Annie's father died when she was ten years old, so she inherited responsibilities that helped to form character and maturity early on.

By now, Annie was a mature young lady. She was wise beyond her years. She had been influenced by her teacher, who prepared her mentally and assured her she had the ability to achieve. Her dream was set to get an education beyond high school, go to college and become a teacher. Her mother, my grandmother, gave me this information during the years I spent around her. My grandmother, Martha, died in 1967, at age 96, after I had graduated from college.

* * * * *

When Annie arrived in Pineland, Texas in September of 1928 to go to high school, she soon adjusted and took her studies very seriously. She worked at her cousin's boarding house where she lived to pay her fee. She washed, cleaned, gathered vegetables from the garden and helped with the cooking. This was an easy adjustment for Annie, she had done all these chores at home.

After two years in Pineland, Annie did not return due to the death of her brother and her mother's illness. She was needed at home to help her sister run the farm. She got into a routine caring for her mother and working the farm. The teacher at the school in town told Annie that more students were attending and that a part-time assistant would be hired. The superintendent gave permission for Annie to assist. Teachers in small, rural places were hard to find. Mrs. Belton was from south Louisiana and did not have a college degree but had attended college. She always dreamed of returning to complete her college education.

Annie went to the school, along the same path she took years earlier, two days a week to assist and teach alongside Mrs. Belton for about three years. She had observed as a young girl and in Pineland that teachers don't just teach. They tend to the building and give food to children who are hungry. Her mother was well again now, and both were discussing her completing her high school certificate. They both agreed that she would be ready to attend a school in one of the closer towns in the state, Many or Mansfield. That way she would be closer to home. Annie chose to go north to Mansfield. She wrote a letter to the principal indicating that she had completed two years in Pineland and had her papers to prove it. Her school record was good; she had passed all classes and taken more than required. She also asked the principal to recommend a place to room. Annie soon received a reply stating the date school would start and with the name of a family that wanted a student to room at their house. She sent a letter to say that she would be coming on the train, the Sunday before school started.

Not knowing anyone in Mansfield, Annie and her mother felt very relieved to get a recommendation from the principal for boarding. At this time, she thought of her father, who would have taken her to the train station in the wagon and would be so proud of her returning to school to complete her high school education. She would catch the train north to Mansfield, which ran once a week on a Sunday in September, 1935.

Annie peered out the window as the conductor announced the upcoming stop. The train began to slow a ways back and came to crawl before stopping. As she stepped off the train she saw a man standing in the back of the small crowd behind the people who would be getting on. The conductor lifted her suitcase and sat it on the ground.

Little did Annie know that where she stepped of the train on her first trip to Mansfield, her home for life would be two miles from the station. She often said, "going to Mansfield was different than going to Pineland. I never, ever forgot coming to Mansfield for the first time."

The man standing behind walked up to Annie, and asked, "are you Annie?" She said, "yes." He said, "I am Mr. Bryant. The principal, Mr. Johnson, selected you to room with me and my family. We are very pleased to have you. I will take care of your luggage. We have a ride in the wagon to our home where my wife and daughter are waiting to meet you. It is nothing fancy, but we try to keep it clean."

As they got closer to the yard, she could see a woman and girl standing. They got out of the wagon. Mrs. Bryant said, "you must be Annie, I'm pleased to meet you. This is our daughter Lillian." Annie replied, "It is good to meet you, and I want to thank you for allowing me to board in your home." Mrs. Bryant replied, "Lillian will show you to the room that the two of you will be sharing together."

Her parents wanted a girl to room with them so that Lillian would have a friend to learn with in high school. Lillian, up to this point, was not overly motivated about school due to some of the difficulties she had experienced.

* * * * *

Mansfield was larger than Pleasant Hill. There was a high school for blacks. There was a boarding house and family homes available for students. There were general stores that sold a variety of merchandise, food, clothing, shoes and farm tools. All items that families needed were purchased at the general store.

* * * * *

On the first day of school Annie and Lillian woke early, got dressed and came to the kitchen for breakfast. They would leave walking to school at half past seven in the morning to get to their classroom doors before eight o'clock. Annie was 11th grade and Lillian was starting 9th.

"When we arrived at school Mr. Johnson was out front directing students to their rooms. He asked the names of the few students he did not know," said Annie, and when I stepped up and said my name was Annie, he said, "the girl from Pleasant Hill. I placed you with a good family. You have a very good record and with good character from Pineland, Texas. I know that you will do well with us and graduate here at DeSoto Parish Training School." Annie said, "yes sir."

There were grades nine, ten and eleven on school grounds comprised of a larger wood building with four classrooms, a bookroom, and small office for the principal. There were also two small wood buildings and two outdoor toilets: one for males and one for females. DeSoto Parish Training School was a state approved senior high school in Louisiana. The term "training" was associated with "black" schools.

With her high school record of classes that came from Pineland, Annie hoped to be able to complete the required curriculum in one year.

She and Lillian walked home together after school. They did chores around the house and helped in the garden. This was nothing new for Annie, she had done these things since grade school.

After chores were finished they helped with dinner. After the kitchen was all cleaned, they used the lamp at the table to complete homework. Annie helped Lillian with her work and explained things she did not understand.

Then the usual ritual before going to bed about nine o'clock.

Annie was pleased and thankful for the room and board arrangement with the Bryants; she was treated and felt like family. In return, she always asked how she could help in addition to her chores.

The school year was going well. She would be able to go home for Christmas this year. She could afford the $1.25 train ride because she had done gardening, washing and cleaning on Saturdays for, Mrs. Howard, an elderly lady that lived down the road from the school. She was given nickels or dimes for work each time.

The year was moving fast, a week from now would be Thanksgiving. A hen had been fattening for the meal. Annie and Lillian would assist Mrs. Bryant in making cornbread dressing, sweet potato pies and collard greens from the garden. A frost had already fallen and southerners swore that collard greens developed an excellent taste and were sweeter once frost had fallen on them.

They had helped to dig the sweet potatoes just a few weeks ago. In the letters she received from her mother, they were doing the same fall harvesting with help from her mother's nephews.

There was something about Annie's experiences as a young girl caring for the chickens that caused her to not like eating chicken. She saw that they pecked and ate anything that came across the yard, they were scavengers. She did not eat chicken until much later, after they were bought in the grocery store. Her daughters recall that she started eating chicken after they left home. The year was moving faster than Annie thought it would. She had written her mother to tell her that Lillian would be coming home with her for Christmas. This was a festive time at school. It reminded her of school at Elizabeth; in every class they sang Christmas carols and talked about family traditions during this season. She and Lillian were now packing their suitcases to go to Pleasant Hill for Christmas. Lillian could hardly contain her excitement. She had never been away from Mansfield.

It was Friday morning, Mr. Bryant had the wagon ready to go to the train station. The train time going south was around eleven thirty.

* * * * *

They unloaded from the wagon, went to the window for "colored" and purchased their tickets. The agent who serviced this window was the same one who serviced the window for "white", he waited on whites first and coloreds last.

The train car for colored was always the first car after the engine locomotive.

The words colored and white were written on bold signs at ticket windows, restrooms, water fountains and all public places.

* * * * *

There were two small villages between Mansfield and Pleasant Hill; the train stopped only if a white cloth was hung on a high pole, which the conductor could see in the distance. The train trip was about two hours.

As the trained rolled closer, Annie shared with Lillian areas with which she was familiar. She knew family names, some were relatives. She could see her school from the train as it got closer.

The train slowed to stop before the station. She could see her cousin Charles in the wagon over at the back of the station yard. Charles knew the social protocol of the era for parking and walking up to meet a passenger. It was the same in Mansfield and all over the south.

Annie and Lillian stepped to the ground from the train, picked up their luggage and walked towards the wagon to meet her cousin. "Hello, Cousin Charles," "Annie, it has been a long time since I saw you. I don't think I know this young lady." "This is Lillian Bryant." "I am pleased to meet you Mr. Charles". Annie said, "I room with Lillian and her parents."

"Yes, Aunt Martha told me that you would be bringing your roommate to visit for Christmas. Lillian, I hope you like the real country out on the farm where Annie and her mother and sister live. You will learn a lot." They all loaded up on the wagon and started out the three miles to the farm. In mid-December the weather was cold and damp. Annie and Lillian wrapped their headscarves tightly, to keep warm, just as they did on cold days walking to school.

The wagon took the same road that she and school mates took when they walked to Elizabeth School, except, the wagon did not go through the quarters. Annie said to Lillian, "we will walk up to town while you are here." Lillian was eager. Annie pointed out houses, gardens with collard greens, patches where sweet potatoes had grown, bare corn and cotton fields.

As the wagon turned left onto the lane to the house, Annie could see her mother standing by the gate waiting to greet them. Annie introduced Lillian to her mother. Martha said to Lillian, "I am pleased to meet you and glad to have you visit." Annie's sister, Mary met them on the front porch. She gave Annie a long hug and shook hands with Lillian.

Once inside they put their things in Annie's room, at the back of the house, then went into the front room to sit by the fireplace. To Annie, the house looked the same, the bedroom behind the front room with the large potbelly heater, her room with a small wood heater that she could heat water in a pan but did not make a fire in her room when she was leaving for school. And the kitchen, next to Annie's room on back of the house, was always a special place. The wood stove gave off plenty heat.

Mary had made beef stew, baked sweet potatoes, collard greens and cornbread for dinner. Dessert was tea cakes and coffee sitting by the fireplace. "Teacakes!" said Annie. Lillian enjoyed the meal as they all sat and told Martha and Mary about school in Mansfield.

During the week Annie was home she introduced Lillian to neighbors, visited friends and relatives, took care of the chickens, gathered eggs, went with Mary to milk the cows, and helped feed the livestock. Lillian pitched in with all the farm chores. They gathered holly branches, with beautiful bright red berries, to decorate the front door of the house for Christmas. Two days before Christmas was the day the baking started. The traditional cakes to be made were pound cake, spice layer cake and coconut layer cake. The fruitcake had been made about two weeks before.

Pies made were pecan, sweet potato, and buttermilk custard. The dinner included chicken, cornbread dressing, potato salad, greens, and homemade yeast rolls.

On the day after Christmas, they walked the route that Annie took as a young girl into town and to Elizabeth School, so that Lillian could get a good view of the area. Lillian commented that Annie had a much longer route to walk than their walk to school in Mansfield.

* * * * *

On the third day after Christmas, Annie and Lillian were taking the train back north to Mansfield to spend New Year's with Lillian's parents and be ready for school after the New Year.

* * * * *

Back to school in the New Year 1937. Near the end of spring, Annie knew that she would graduate in May. Graduation was held in the school auditorium on May 13, 1937, at eight o'clock p.m. The program proceeded with the address given by Dr. J.S. Clark, President of Southern University.

* * * * *

After the address, Mr. Johnson presented certificates to each graduate.

Annie kept this certificate, throughout her life, in the place where special documents were stored.

High School Diploma Received May 13, 1937

The next day after graduation Annie packed her suitcase and got her things together to return to Pleasant Hill. Mr. and Mrs. Johnson had asked her to come by the school before she left. They congratulated her on graduating and told her they would like to help her get a teaching job in DeSoto Parish. They knew that she already had some teaching experience from Sabine Parish and would be returning to teach there.

They emphasized that from DeSoto Parish she could begin working towards her bachelor's degree and take college classes when they were offered.

The Faculty and Senior Class

of the

DeSoto Parish Training School

request the honor of your presence

at their

Graduating Exercises

to be held in

School Auditorium

Thursday Evening, May Thirteenth

Nineteen hundred thirty-seven

at 8 P. M.

Mansfield, Louisiana

High School Graduation Program, 1937

CLASS ROLL

Allen, Verna Bernice
Austin, Jessie Belle
Brown, Zadie Janice
Charles, Edythe Hortense
Edwards, Eula Mae
Fobbs, Clara Syrenia

Garlington, Sataria Ethel

Gaulden, Reuben Lazelle
Guiton, Maudice Odessa
Hall, Ollie Mae
Henderson, Julia Faye
Hooks, Cenell Jerlean
Jones, Paul Jonathan
Morris, James Randolph

McBride, Breman Odysses
Roundtree, Preston LaRue
Redley, Herman Lee
Richardson, Arthur DeVanter
Simpkins, Buford Lecester
Washington, Zora LeVonne
Williams, Annie Berdine

MOTTO:
The End Crowns the Work

CLASS COLORS:
Orchid and Yellow

CLASS FLOWER:
Sweet Peas

High School Graduation Program, 1937

16

PROGRAM

PROCESSIONAL

INVOCATION .... REV. J. H. Fobbs

FEMALE SEXTETTE: Roses of Picardy .... Weatherly

SALUTATORY: The End Crowns the Work................. Clara Fobbs

DUET: Ah! Sweet Mystery of Life .... Herbert

VALEDICTORY: The Value of Industrial

                Education.... .... Zora Lee Washington

GLEE CLUB: Gypsy Love Song .... Herbert

ADDRESS .... Dr. J. S. Clark,

           President, Southern University, Scotlandville, Louisiana.

TRIO: Who Knows? .... Dressler

PRESENTATION OF DIPLOMAS

CLASS SONG

RECESSIONAL

BENEDICTION

High School Graduation Program, 1937

Young Teacher and College Years

1937-1949

Historical Point:

In 1937, among the few colleges in Louisiana that blacks could attend, Annie attended Southern University, Baton Rouge, Louisiana and Grambling College, Grambling, Louisiana.

Classes were offered on a limited schedule; one or two per session. At the time, the teaching curriculum was a two-year program. Completion was a long process because of the limited availability of classes. Annie enrolled in her first college classes in summer 1937. Summers of 1937, 1938, and spring of 1939 were extension classes offered by Southern University.

Annie enrolled at Grambling College and took classes summers 1939-42 and 1946-49. During the years 1943-1946, we will learn later in this biography why Annie did not take classes.

Some of the classes Annie took, during the summers that helped her gain knowledge in teaching were: Class Management, Labor Problems, Rural Life Problems and Elementary Nutrition.

Classes were motivational and offered knowledge in the profession.

From this beginning of post high school education, classes were taken during summer sessions and on Saturday mornings. Teachers would carpool together to take a class. *When news got out that a class in education was offered, it was like hearing about the gold rush.*

Not all teachers were eager to take college classes, they were in a comfort zone they didn't want interrupted. Others married, had children, cared for elderly parents and worked on family farms for survival. Still others had managed to finish high school but had to help their family as tenant farmers in sharecropping (to work **land** for a share of the crop). They taught in the community and managed to take a class when they could.

Annie saw more opportunity in DeSoto Parish. She had also been told that she would have a teaching job in Sabine Parish. Her goal for a long time was to become an elementary teacher. She liked observing children learn and helping them understand.

* * * * *

Annie returned to Pleasant Hill after high school graduation and summer college classes in 1937. She resumed all responsibilities on the family farm, working in the garden, harvesting beans, peas, corn, watermelons, picking blackberries, plums. She "chopped" cotton. Annie often remarked that she was thankful to have a mother, sister, a cousin, and nephews to share the work. She could never really learn to master "milking a cow." So there were others to do it. But she loved milk, especially buttermilk, which she drank all her life. She was known by family and friends for making buttermilk biscuits. She often wondered what it would be like if her father had lived to see her grow up.

In late summer she was offered a teaching job at Elizabeth School, teaching the older students. Deep down in her soul, Annie wanted to teach in DeSoto Parish, however, she felt that she owed something to Sabine, the place that molded her. All the other social and racial constraints remained unchanged. Annie had observed her teachers in Mansfield. There was something about this year that stood out with her as a teacher. Pleasant Hill was a small rural town. The two largest family groups were the Scotts and Owens. She was related to both. Her maternal grandfather was a Scott and her maternal grandmother was an Owens. She soon recognized the added challenges of teaching in a school community where almost everybody was kin to you. She was accused of showing favoritism to some relatives over others. *She often shared this situation: She had given a language test, two synonyms, pear and pare were called. "When I called pear—I said "a fruit we eat that grows on trees"-when I called pare_ I said "to peel with a knife." One student got the words (number and definition specific) correctly. Another student got the wrong words (number and definition). Annie wrote on paper with wrong words that they were wrong but spelled correctly. Consequently, one score was better than the other. Annie was accused of favoring the cousin who made the better grade.*

* * * * *

These were early lessons learned as a young teacher. Annie had a good year teaching in her hometown. So many were proud of her. Only she and one other person, a gentleman, had achieved to be able to return and teach. He taught for many years and when Pleasant Hill got a high school for blacks, he became principal.

In early spring, Annie wrote a letter to the Johnsons at DeSoto Parish Training School. She indicated that she would be interested in returning to continue college classes and teach. Also, that she wanted to work in the northern part of the parish. She had numerous relatives that lived in the southern part of DeSoto Parish, adjacent to Sabine.

By the end of May as school closed, Annie received a letter from Mrs. Johnson stating that she would have a position in rural Pine Ridge; located in north central DeSoto Parish. Annie wrote to a family recommended to her by Mrs. Johnson to communicate that she was the new teacher and needed a place to stay.

Historical Point

In segregated America, the black teacher was the most highly respected and revered person in the community. Most teachers lived in the communities where they worked, the people looked up to them. Some communities had a teacher from that area. With their leadership they organized very strong Parent Teacher Associations. Black schools relied mostly on the interests and efforts of the community. Out of this relationship schools were assisted with hot lunches, firewood, water tanks, (for gathering and storing rain water) and other equipment. Good Human Relations were critical for a teacher in establishing herself. Annie had the character for inspiring and working with people.

In the black community, it was an honor for the teacher to room and board in a family's home. There were one or two families who had the modest accommodations to house the teacher. Usually this

was a couple who did not have children or their children had grown up and left home.

* * * * *

Annie took the train north to Mansfield in late August. This time she had a trunk and suitcase packed with things to start her career. She would not return home until Christmas. Mr. Bryant picked her up in the wagon and would take her out to Pine Ridge (about ten miles) on the next morning.

Annie was delighted to see the Bryant's and to spend a little time with Lillian, who was preparing to go to Chicago to live with an aunt to work and finish high school. Next morning the Bryant's drove Annie out to Pine Ridge. It was August, leaving early allowed plenty of time to return home before dark.

Richard and Alice Reed had opened their home for the new teacher. The men unloaded the trunk and suitcase off the wagon. Annie's room was spacious enough, located in the front of the house with bathroom (no indoor plumbing) outside her door. There was a quilting room next to hers and the Reed's bedroom was in the back of the house off the kitchen. That reminded her of her room at home. Mrs. Reed had prepared a summer dinner of purple-hull peas with fat-back, corn, chow-chow, fried okra and cornbread. Dessert was blackberry dumplings.

After the meal Annie said goodbye to the Bryant's. She wished Lillian much luck in Chicago and promised to stay in touch. Annie and Lillian remained friends throughout their adult lives, mostly by letter and Lillian's infrequent visits to Louisiana to see her parents.

They spent time together some years later when Lillian came to Mr. Bryant's funeral. Mrs. Bryant went back to Chicago with Lillian and passed away two years later.

* * * * *

Annie discussed some housekeeping matters and told Mrs. Reed that starting at this moment, she would have her share of the chores. She helped to clean the kitchen. That evening they talked and got to know more about each other. Mrs. Reed was talented in sewing and quilting. She promised the new teacher a quilt made just for her. They told her about the families and children in the community. She asked questions; they answered. She told them that she would walk the community and go door to door to meet the parents and children. The following day Annie got up had breakfast and started out on her walk on the route to the school, meeting children she would be teaching. The school building at Pine Ridge was a two-room unpainted building, much like Elizabeth School in Pleasant Hill. Books were stacked on wooden shelves in the back room. Large book charts stood in the corner. All furniture was wooden and was made by men in the community. The furniture was a standard size. For some students the desks and chairs fit, for others they were too small or too large. Student desks and chairs were stacked on one side of the room.

A few children had already gathered at the school door to meet the new teacher. They asked, "are you our new teacher?" Annie said, "yes, my name is Miss Williams, and I am your new teacher." She observed the smiles and sighs on their faces.

When the teacher came into the community to start the school year, there was not a problem getting help cleaning, setting up, organizing and running errands.

School started within a week of Annie's arrival in Pine Ridge. But, for her, the work started as soon as she arrived. There were about twenty-five students ranging in grades one through six. There was no pre-school or kindergarten. The challenges, for the black teacher, during this period were enormous. They had very little to work with, but they had passion as they saw situations they could make better.

Annie's first year teaching in DeSoto Parish was challenging but successful. She survived by combining her experience, knowledge from college classes and using common sense in working with people. She developed this strategy for the remainder of her career. Pine Ridge was an isolated area where people were thirsty for activities, involvement and leadership. The people in the community were cooperative, positive, and participated. School started in September. However, during that era many families and their children worked as share-croppers or worked on farms. Students in the deep south could not start school until crops; sweet potatoes, peanuts, sugar cane were finished, including cotton picked.

Most black families did the best they could in getting their children to school. Some children came to school on a staggered basis. One of the responsibilities of the teacher was to make sure that students came to school. Annie carefully recorded the names of students who reported to school. She asked students for the names of students who had not come to school. She would announce, "tell all students who have not reported to school to come." Annie compiled a list of names of students that had not come to school. She walked the community during evenings to talk to parents. Annie always encouraged parents to send children to school, even before attendance was mandatory. She knew that if the teacher and the parent did not care about the child's education, nobody else would.

Annie knew that some students did not have decent clothes to wear. In hot, humid Louisiana during summer, children went barefoot and scantily covered their bodies.

Historical Point

When black colleges started in Louisiana in the early 1900's they were Industrial and Agricultural Schools. In 1901 Grambling was founded as The Colored Industrial and Agricultural School. In 1905 the school moved to its present location and was renamed North Louisiana Agricultural and Industrial School.

- *1936, the curriculum at Grambling shifted to rural teacher education.*
- *1944, the first baccalaureate degree was awarded in elementary education*
- *1946 the school became Grambling College*
- *1949 the college earned its first accreditation by the Southern Association of Colleges and Schools*
- *1949 Annie B. Williams Adams received the Bachelor of Science in Elementary Education*

As we have seen from history, it was difficult for black women to get an education in the rural south. There were more opportunities up north and in cities.

It was a privilege to graduate from high school and take college classes. When school closed in May, teachers were off to take classes in the summer and returning to teach in the fall. It took a long time for teachers to get their degrees. There they met other

future educators from rural places and towns who had the same experiences. Some of them became lifetime friends.

* * * * *

The summer of 1939 was the first summer that Annie went away to continue her quest for a college education. Living on campus in the dormitory was akin to being with family at home, most things were done community style-washing, ironing, cleaning and cooking. On Saturday mornings they washed clothes and hung them on lines to dry, inside the dormitory. There was a cook in the small cafeteria. Students were assigned a day in the cafeteria to assist the cook in the preparation of all meals; peeling potatoes, making bread, frying, baking, placing food in large serving bowls, setting the table and cleaning the kitchen.

One dish they frequently prepared in the college cafeteria was "baked apples." This was the first dish that Annie taught her girls to make. Baked apples remain a popular breakfast food on their menus.

Annie told the story so many times of how they ate table style, at a long table and passed the serving dishes. She often said to her daughters, when they were in college in the sixties, "table style worked in the thirties, because people did not overeat during those times." This was just like families serving themselves at special meal gatherings.

* * * * *

During those years the parish supervisor would make random assignments so that schools with ample numbers of students would have a teacher. Sometimes a very small community with five or six children did not get a teacher, but had to walk or take a wagon to the nearest school where there was a teacher. Students from a long distance could not come every day; so the teacher would give books with assignments for them to bring when they came.

Annie frequently quoted," black teachers were challenged beyond reason in educating students, they had to deal with poverty, Jim Crow laws, hunger and all the ills of society during those times."

Using the knowledge learned from classes and experiences, her natural passion was to help children. She collected used clothes and shoes, she asked seamstresses to make clothing items with leftover cloth scraps.

* * * * *

One of the most blatant injustices of the time was what teachers were paid. **Black teachers did not get the same pay as white teachers.**

Annie was paid thirty-five dollars per month in 1937; fifty dollars per month in 1941. A white teacher was paid one hundred twenty dollars or more per month. And with these salaries, white teachers were given more supplies and materials.

Annie's annual salary in 1971, the year she retired, was eighty-seven hundred dollars. Do the calculation.

Other injustices were:

- Black teachers were not granted a leave of absence for illness or other family matters
- Black teachers were told not to get pregnant or wait ten years to get pregnant
- Black teachers had to attend parish in-service meetings on Saturday.

* * * * *

Through the late forties things remained "status quo" in educating black children. All was rural education in various assignments. Annie stated, "I taught all subjects, so, in addition to what I learned in college classes, I had to read to gain information in the subjects taught. I roomed in the community, went home to Pleasant Hill at Christmas, returned for the spring semester and went to college during summers." That was the pattern for almost a decade as she continued to pursue her college degree.

* * * * *

Annie was returning from Pleasant Hill in January 1941 on a cold, rainy day. When she got off the train in Mansfield she saw a lady preparing to board train and a gentleman helping her with her luggage. As she exited and passed the waiting passengers, they exchanged greetings. She was now living with Mr. and Mrs. Gilliam, a middle-aged couple in another area near Pine Ridge. She peered out and did not see Mr. Gilliam in the wagon. Passengers boarded the train.

She noticed a gentleman approaching her. He asked, "are you Miss Williams? She said," yes, I am." He said, "How are you? I am Roosevelt Adams. Mr. Gilliam asked me to drive you to their home today." I live in the Morning Glory community. He knew that I'd be coming here to bring my sister, to catch the train." Annie said, "I am Annie Williams, I'm pleased to meet you." When I did not see Mr. Gilliam's wagon, I wondered how I'd get out there in all this cold rainy weather.

Roosevelt said that "Mr. Gilliam had not felt well lately. He knew I would be coming to the station today and asked me to pick you up." Mr. Gilliam knew that Roosevelt would get Annie to their home safely.

After loading Annie's suitcase on to the wagon, they started out from the station through South Mansfield out to the country road toward Pine Ridge. As they traveled out of town the unyielding clay road slowed the wagon down as it rolled through the mud bumps and wet puddles. Roosevelt said, "the roads are muddy, it will take longer, but I will get you there." During that wagon trip Annie and Roosevelt got to know more about the other. He had known that she was a teacher in Pine Ridge. He learned on that trip that she was single, as was he.

On this ride, Annie and Roosevelt talked about each other's families. He told her the lady at the train station was his sister, who was a teacher in Shreveport. Roosevelt told Annie that he had heard of Miss Williams, the teacher in Pine Ridge and teachers in other nearby communities. He said, "parents like the way you teach their children, that you really want them to learn."

Where Annie lived now was closer to the school than where she lived before. They finally made their way to the Gilliam home. After they arrived, he took her suitcase into the house.

Mrs. Gilliam had a delicious dinner of tomato okra stew, cornbread, and pork cracklins (the fried skin of the hog). Mrs. Gilliam made a pot of coffee and took out fruitcake left over from the holidays. Annie had brought holiday leftovers also. She opened a package with her sister's spice cake. They enjoyed the coffee and cake. Meals in the winter consisted of canned fruits and vegetables, salted meats, biscuits or cornbread.

Roosevelt said that he must leave to get back to his home before dark in the wagon. All agreed he should get started. He said to Annie "I would like to visit you in two weeks, if that is okay." Annie replied, "yes, and that it would have to be on Sunday afternoon." Social visits during that time were usually on Sunday after church.

* * * * *

This meeting of all parties on this date formed life relationships. Mr. and Mrs. Gilliam were a couple. Due to the bad weather, Mr. Gilliam thought a younger man could handle a wagon and horses, so he asked Roosevelt. Annie always thought that Mr. Gilliam probably felt okay, but thoughtfully planned and set up this opportunity for them to meet. Annie and Roosevelt, both single, met and started a friendship.

In a conversation later in the evening, Annie and Mrs. Gilliam talked about the news, happenings and events that occurred during the holidays. There was nothing out of the ordinary. Annie welcomed new children that came after holidays, but it made her sad to lose students without saying a proper goodbye.

Mrs. Gilliam asked her about Roosevelt. She said, "I've known his family for years. They are nice people. There are six girls and four boys. Roosevelt is the youngest. I know that you are an eligible lady and to add to that a young teacher. So many of the single men are interested." She went on to name ones in the community to stay away from, young and old. Annie listened intently and heeded the advice. The information from that conversation was consistent with what Annie had learned from her upbringing. It taught her to think and carefully weigh major life decisions. She had made decisions prior to this regarding her life. Her long-range goal was to teach and get a college degree.

Annie and Roosevelt continued their friendship on the Sunday afternoon visits. Roosevelt assisted Annie in getting to the train station to go to her classes at Grambling that semester. During the summer Annie stayed on campus. After summer school was over Annie went to Pleasant Hill to spend time with her mother and sister. Roosevelt came down to meet them. They liked him instantly.

After Annie returned to Pine Ridge in early September, Roosevelt took her to meet his family. She often said, "that was a large crowd, his family." They were happy to meet.

The year 1941 went fast. The courtship developing between Annie and Roosevelt was very strong now. The fall season brought the start of school and the usual activities. Annie became involved in local activities and continued her classes. When the teacher visited a church, they were recognized, ushered to a seat in the front and asked to speak. This pattern was the catalyst that started her popularity as a speaker at churches and organizations. This pattern continued all of Annie's teaching career and throughout retirement. The black teacher was held in high esteem. Annie used this opportunity to encourage parents to support the school and help their children learn. She had begun to see the community improve.

* * * * *

As Thanksgiving was approaching, one Sunday, Roosevelt came to visit. He said to Annie, "you are the one I have chosen to be my wife. Let us visit your mother and my parents during Thanksgiving. I would like to ask Miss Martha for your hand in marriage." Annie was delighted but not overwhelmed. She had gotten to know Roosevelt over these months and saw that he had a strong work ethic, he was caring, and from a loving family.

The practice during this time was to ask parents for permission to marry a female. We often asked our mother what would happen if the parents said no.

After Thanksgiving, all was okay, they were officially engaged with blessings from both families.

Marriage and Family

Annie and Roosevelt were married on January 11, 1942, in Pleasant Hill, at her family home on the farm. The minister who officiated the ceremony was Reverend Fobbs. Ironically, he pastored both churches where they were members, Morning Glory in Mansfield, and Antioch in Pleasant Hill. He knew both families well and thought the two of them had made a good selection and would succeed in marriage and life. Well, he was right, they were married 61 years when Roosevelt died in 2003.

* * * * *

Annie Williams Adams, married January 11, 1942

Roosevelt Adams, married January 11, 1942

After they were married, they returned to Mansfield, roomed with a relative until they found a house. Within a week they rented a three room "shot gun" house in Park Place, a black area adjacent to town near the "ice plant" and "foundry", a steel plant. They remained at this location about four years. Because she came from a family that owned a farm, Annie never believed in renting or living on heir property. She and Roosevelt worked and saved their money so they could purchase a home. In 1947, Annie and Roosevelt purchased their home about two miles from the train station in South Mansfield. They rebuilt the home in 1949 to a six-room wooden structure. The rooms were living, dining, kitchen, three bedrooms and indoor bath. It was painted white with dark green shutters.

They purchased their first car that year; a 1939 chevrolet. He drove Annie out to Pine Ridge on Monday mornings and picked her up on Friday. Annie continued to room with the Gilliams through her tenure at Pine Ridge. During the early 1940's travel was not convenient. Roads were not developed and just a few were maneuverable by car. The Gilliams home was on a road, however, most homes were miles off the main road; you parked the car and walked across fields to houses. To get to Roosevelt's family home you had to park the car on the road and walk a quarter mile to the house. You could see the house from where the car was parked. To get to Annie's family home you turned off the main road and drove about a half mile down the lane that bordered the property. This was the same route Annie walked to school as a young girl.

Things were "progressing along" as Annie would say.

* * * * *

Annie remained at Pine Ridge for two more years. She enrolled in classes at Grambling, during spring and summer sessions. Now that she lived in Mansfield and they had a car, it was more convenient for her to get to the train station.

Annie and her family had never owned a car on the farm. Roosevelt's father had purchased a car. Both families were excited but Annie's family was overly excited. They would drive to Pleasant Hill usually one weekend of the month. They would take Annie's sister and mother riding. It was so exciting to go around the little town, stop to say hello to some and wave at others. Cars were rare in the forties.

* * * * *

Annie was on maternity leave part of 1943 and 1945. She did not take classes at Grambling from 1943-1945; she resumed taking classes in summer 1946. She received the Bachelor of Science in Elementary in August, 1949. She was assigned to Good Hope in Frierson during the years 1943-1948 and returned to full-time teaching. After her return, she never took a leave for any reason. She taught continuously until she retired in 1971.

Mid Teaching Years

1950-1960

SCHOOL DAYS
1949 - 50

*Annie Williams Adams Principal Longstreet
Rosenwald Elementary School*

Her assignment was Principal at Longstreet, in 1949, with two other teachers. During this era of education, the elementary principal taught a class, usually sixth grade. By now Annie and her girls went to school together. They learned to get up early, dress, eat breakfast and get in the car. They had responsibilities for packing snacks and filling the water cooler. They left home on Monday morning, returned on Wednesday and Friday. They roomed in a house next to the school for teachers. As principal, Annie often had to stay late and take care of issues related to running the school. The girls were trained, very young, how to cope and adjust to situations with their mother's work. The car was the library, workplace with coloring books, crayons, readers, dolls, snacks, and water. It was during these years that Annie had her own young children as a teacher. She was always so proud of her two little girls and could not wait for them to start school. She always said she would take them to school with her. She was blessed to have both families as babysitters when needed.

In 1950, Annie was assigned principal of Howard Point, a large community a few miles out from Mansfield. There were three teachers. This had been a goal for her supervisor to get her an assignment close to home where she could commute each day. This was the closest she had ever worked from her home in Mansfield. Howard Point community was adjacent to Clear Lake (still exists) and spread over a large area. Some students were bussed, because of the distance. Most students walked up to three miles on the red clay gravel road to the school.

This area, more than any place she had taught, reminded her of Pleasant Hill. The school was close to a Mahaw Bog, a large one. In spring the teachers were given buckets of mahaws and some parents sent jelly. The men picked buckets of mahaws to sell alongside the road near the lake.

Annie remembered teaching students under the mahaw bog in the 1930's in Pleasant Hill. In one of her classes, she learned that students are successful at learning when they can interact with the environment. Annie prepared her sixth graders for a trip (fieldtrip) to the mahaw bog behind the school in April, just at the time the berries were ripening. Each student was to collect a handful of berries and place in the bucket. While observing, Annie pointed out; color of berries, thorns, size, trees under large trees, swamp like ground and denseness of mahaw plants.

The lake was also a wonderful resource for freshwater fish in the community. Nonetheless, Annie still saw hunger with families. She had always remembered what she learned in a college class in 1940, *Rural Life Problems.* With her studies and experience she was more equipped to deal with situations that impacted the education of students. She was not reticent about offering suggestions to improve family life.

Annie had been teaching over a decade now. School buildings were old, leaky, and drafty, some new books, but secondhand books were still sent out to black schools. Annie had seen a demonstration of copying materials and tests for students in a college class. The copier was a wooden tablet with sides. A liquid substance was mixed and poured into tablet which congealed like jello. The assignment or test questions were handwritten on a white carbon page. The carbon page was laid on the substance. Once the imprint was soaked into the substance from the master page, white sheets were pressed by hand, and imprinted. The color was purple on white paper. Annie purchased the copier for use with her students.

The biggest improvement that she saw was hot school lunches. It was up to the principal in each school to find a cook in the community, and work with the school district administration to start a hot lunch program. That she did, because she knew how critical it was for a child to have nutrition to learn.

Annie was told that the children would have to bring bowls and spoons to get hot lunch. She and her supervisor met with the superintendent. She stated the hygiene problem that would cause and that most children would not be able to bring a dish to use because they did not have dishes. She said, "children come to school hungry, all are entitled to a hot lunch, which is sometimes their only decent meal." Utensils were issued to the school for student lunches.

She could detect when a child was hungry. She often said she saw hunger in school children from her first teaching job in 1937 to her retirement, in 1971.

Hunger was still as prevalent or more so, as when she was a girl. She would often say "hunger is worse now than when I grew up. Whether or not it was peanuts or plums, we always had something to eat, living on a farm." Annie was now packing snacks for her girls but continued to keep a stash of snacks for a hungry child.

The cook at Howard Point, Mrs. Thomas, lived across the field and had a view of the school grounds. She was a southern comfort food cook. She made all the typical foods you can imagine that would "water-your-mouth" from childhood. When she cooked the Thanksgiving dinner of turkey, cornbread dressing, candied yams and trimmings, people in the community came to purchase a lunch. Annie's supervisor would go to at least two schools to get dinner; she would often come to Howard Point.

Annie had to make administrative decisions every day. In preparation for a large Thanksgiving meal, she had to select the substitute cook, another kitchen helper, to come in and assist with such a huge dinner. Annie helped to serve on that day and others depending on the meal. Annie had her apron that hung in the kitchen closet, when needed.

Annie learned early on that the principal had to pitch in and do many things to assure the on-going progress of the school; she never hesitated. Her attitude was to do what it takes to get the job done.

In the rural schools boys played basketball. They would play other schools in May when the weather was warm and sunny. One day a sixth-grade girl asked, "Mrs. Adams why can't girls play basketball like the boys. I am good and can play." She named other girls who could and wanted to play.

This was a defining moment in Annie's career. That night she could not sleep for thinking of the request for girls to form a basketball team. She thought to deny girls to play would be akin to the same social limitations that existed in society. She concluded that girls should be given the opportunity to express themselves through basketball. On the playground all these years, boys played on one side, girls on the other, girls and boys had separate lines. She knew that girls and boys performed in the classroom, so she thought, why not. She contacted principals in the surrounding schools, they all thought it was a great idea. They organized teams of girls. She discussed with her 6th grade class that girls could play when the team played other schools. The girls' basketball team was organized at Howard Point and all the girls teams performed excellently.

At that time in education, in 1952, Annie and her colleagues would never have dreamed of Title IX being implemented twenty years later.

Historical Point

Title IX became a federal law in 1972 and ensures that females have equal access to athletic opportunities.

Annie pursued graduate work much the same as she did undergraduate studies, summers and weekends. Black teachers were not granted sabbatical leave to study for degrees. Annie started graduate studies in summer of 1955 and completed the Master of Science in Elementary Education, from Texas Southern University, Houston, Texas in August 1960.

Master of Science in Elementary Education

Later Teaching Years-Retirement

1961-1971

School Consolidation was one of the major changes taking place in rural education starting in the mid 1950's. Rural schools had one, two and three teachers during this time. Small isolated rural schools were closed and moved to a campus for grades 1-12. In rural areas today, these pre-school through high school campuses still exist. In DeSoto Parish, Louisiana, the bulk of the consolidation of schools took place between 1954-58. Teachers in the small schools were reassigned to the 1-12 campus to which their school was moved. Yes, Moved! In many cases small school buildings were relocated, others were too dilapidated to move, they were torn down. Howard Point was consolidated in 1955, the building was demolished.

Annie was assigned to Second Ward High School (Grades 1-12) in fall of 1955, as a sixth-grade teacher. She welcomed the change. There was an advantage to working on a large campus. ***This was the first time, twenty years into Annie's career, that a school had electricity, refrigeration and indoor toilets.*** Numerous other schools had been consolidated and brought to this campus. This was a reassignment (coming together) of students and teachers from different communities in a section of the parish. There was one principal for this organization. There was no assistant principal, counselor, speech therapist or reading specialist. Each classroom teacher had to perform the duties of these professionals as the need arose in their classrooms. Annie felt here as a teacher, for the first time, that she had more opportunity to focus on children. She brought children home with her to spend the night, after her daughters were gone off to college. These were memorable experiences for students.

The advantages for belonging to this type of school organization or being in a setting with a group of teachers at a large campus were having a support group and the exchange of information, dealing with classroom issues, students, sharing materials and teaching lessons.

Also, when a teacher was absent or late, the teacher in the adjoining classroom could watch the class and get them started on classwork. At the high school campus teachers attended basketball games, choir concerts and graduation.

Many of these teachers who now came together at one campus had known each other for years. Some were close friends, relatives, and others professional acquaintances. They had traveled together and encouraged each other over the years taking classes at Grambling.

The Louisiana Education Association was formed for white teachers only. Annie was a member of the Louisiana Colored Teachers Association (LCTA). The LCTA was organized so that black teachers could be active participants and function freely in a professional organization. The LCTA helped teachers deal with all the things in this biography that teachers had to deal with in the rural schools. Black teachers embraced and supported this organization. The LCTA later changed its name to Louisiana Education Association.

Annie was a lifelong member of Louisiana Education Association and later National Education Association.

In the late sixties and early seventies many of the rural Black women teachers of Louisiana that started teaching in the 1930's were retiring. Even with a lack of resources, low pay and dilapidated conditions, Annie and her colleagues remained dedicated to raising the level of the students and communities. They were nurturers, diplomats, mediators, counselors, friends, daughters, sisters, wives, and mothers.

Annie was tenacious, courageous, and determined.

Reflection

In her groundbreaking book, <u>A Voice From the South</u>, the great African American educator, Anna Julia Cooper, wrote that "Only the BLACK WOMAN [sic] can say 'when and where I enter, in the quiet, undisputed dignity of my womanhood, without violence and without suing or special patronage, then and there the whole *Negro race enters with me* [sic].'"[1]

Cooper, in this unapologetically inclusive statement, is positioning black women as the social justice vanguard for not just racial equality, but gender equality as well. Cooper understood the significance of what black women themselves represent and the indispensability of their contributions to American society in which the notion of democracy is selectively applied.

In 2005, when I was working on my Master of Arts in History, I interviewed Annie B. Adams for my thesis project on the work of black women educators in rural Louisiana during the 1930's and 1940's. The ninety-two year-old Adams took the time to discuss the importance of the work she had done as an elementary educator for more than 30 years in the pre-Civil Rights Movement south. She was an invaluable resource for my project, and she was also my grandmother. Outside of the obvious familial connection, I was drawn to the work that she and so many other countless black women embarked upon in the rural south at such an uncertain moment in United States history. What I sensed in those conversations with my grandmother was the very essence of what Anna Julia Cooper articulated in her 1892 work, that Black women represent the very embodiment of democratic inclusion in the American experiment.

---

[1] Cooper, Anna Julia. *A Voice From the South*. New York: Oxford University Press, 1988. Reprint. Originally published: Xenia, Ohio: Aldine Printing House, 1892.

As Cooper reminds us, black women, who are essentially the cornerstones of African American communities, represent the struggle against racial and gender inequities (along with class inequity) that have for so long haunted the American social fabric, and it's when these women progress that the whole of the black community progresses with them. In Cooper's, <u>A Voice From the South</u>, she also profoundly emphasizes the importance of education, linking it with African American social uplift. When I first encountered Cooper's book, my grandmother was foremost in my mind. As a black woman educator in the rural south, for me, my grandmother's work is not only a testament to Cooper's call for uplift, but also an inspiration for my own work. When asked why she entered the profession, my grandmother stated, "I was glad to get the job of teaching because I wanted to work and I was just proud to go."[2] It's because of a long line of African American women trailblazers that I am able to progress as an African American woman today; and furthermore, it's with love and admiration that I honor my grandmother by serving in the teaching profession as my chosen life's work. I only hope that I can represent the fortitude and perserverance that my grandmother represented for me and for her community.

Cynara Robinson
September 12, 2015

---

[2] Mrs. Annie B. Adams, interview by author, tape recording, Mansfield, Louisiana, 24 October 2004.

SCHOOL DAYS 1962-63
SECOND WARD

Annie Williams Adams Teacher Second Ward High School 1962-63

Second Ward High School, DeSoto Parish, Louisiana was an all-black segregated high school during 1950's through 1980's. The school was closed due to desegregation. An extraordinary setting where black teachers had expectations for learning and caring.

Annie Williams Adams retired from SWHS in 1971.

She is pictured: second row, second from right

Photo by McPhearson

STATE DEPARTMENT OF EDUCATION

Added 9/22/60;
Master of Education degree,
Texas Southern University,
1960.

Mildred Baird
SUPERVISOR OF CERTIFICATION

OF LOUISIANA

Type A. (Negro) Valid for Life for Continuous Service

No. 335

This Certificate is issued to Annie B. Williams Adams

by the State Department of Education of Louisiana, based upon the following requirements:

Degree B. S., Grambling College, 1942   Professional Training 43 semester hours

Experience   11 years   Subjects and Services Specified:

Eligibility: This certificate authorizes the employment of the holder to teach only those subjects and/or to engage in other services specified on the certificate.

Elementary grades

Baton Rouge, La.,   September 12,   19 42.

Jeth Williams
Supervisor of Teacher Education and Certification

Shelby M. Jackson
State Superintendent of Education

Longstreet Rosenwald Elementary School
Longstreet, Louisiana
Built 1924
The old building stands in 2021 as a community center.
It is part of Louisiana trust for Historic Preservation

The Rosenwald Schools was a building program, partially funded by philanthropist Julius Rosenwald and partnered with Booker T. Washington, an African American educator, who managed the program.

The Rosenwald Schools were often the first schools in a black community. The community had to donate money to match a grant from the Rosenwald school building program. Other donations from the community were labor and materials.

The Louisiana Rosenwald Schools for African American students were in mostly rural areas constructed between 1912 and 1932.

Longstreet Rosenwald Elementary, Longstreet, Louisiana, was constructed in 1924.

Annie Williams Adams was the principal at Longstreet Elementary in 1949-50.

GRAMBLING STATE UNIVERSITY
OFFICE OF ALUMNI AFFAIRS

POST OFFICE BOX 60
GRAMBLING, LA 71245

(318) 247-7056
(318) 247-6708
Fax (318) 247-7046

March 29, 1999

Mrs. Annie W. Adams
Post Office Box 698
Mansfield, LA 71052

Dear Mrs. Adams:

President Steve A. Favors, Administrators, Academic Deans, Department Heads, Faculty, Staff and Students **INVITE YOU** to join the University Family in celebrating your Fiftieth Anniversary Class Reunion the weekend of May 22-23, 1999. Saturday, May 22, 1999 a Mid-Day Luncheon along with several other activities have been planned for your enjoyment. Sunday, May 23, 1999 you will participate in the Commencement Exercises. During the commencement exercises, members of the Class of 1949 will be awarded special recognition in conjunction with their Fiftieth Class Reunion. You are a member of the sixth (four-year) class to have the honor of being a **PROUD GRAMBLINITE OF 50 YEARS.**

Fifty years ago you graduated from Grambling College, now known as Grambling State University, your Alma Mater. For many years, as a GRAMBLINITE, you have represented your Alma Mater well. Grambling has benefited by having you as an ambassador who has contributed to the **well-being** of others through your profession and as a citizen in your community. Grambling State University is **recognized** throughout the State of Louisiana, the Region, the Nation and the World for its depth and integrity in academia. A few of GSU's academic strengths include degrees in the major disciplines, two professional schools (Nursing and Social Work), and programs at the masters and doctoral levels.

Grambling **continues** to be **recognized** as the HOME BASE for the preparation of qualified, competent teachers and retains prideful prowess in athletics, the marching band, musical groups and the choir. The recently established Earl Lester Cole Honors College (1990) is well known as a strong participating member of the State, Regional and National Honors Systems. GSU is a member of the National Student Exchange (NSE).

The Grambling family looks forward to your participation. We are making special arrangements for you during the **Fiftieth Anniversary Class Reunion Weekend** and need your help. Enclosed is a tentative schedule of events; however, completion of the plans depend on your response.

A Member of the University of Louisiana System
An Equal Opportunity Employer and Educational Facilities Accessible To The Disabled

Mrs. Adams
March 29, 1999
Page -2-

Read carefully each enclosure and **return the registration form on or before Friday, April 23, 1999**. We look forward to hearing from you. Your achievement is great and **deserves recognition**. We wish to celebrate with you.

A Fifty-Year Class Reunion is a "Once in a Lifetime Opportunity."

Sincerely,

Helen Richards-Smith/es

Helen Richards-Smith, Coordinator
Fiftieth Class Reunion of 1949

Vickie D. Joe

Vickie D. Joe
Assistant Director of Alumni Affairs
Co-Coordinator, Fiftieth Reunion Committee

HRS/es

Enclosures

xc: Dr. Herbert Simmons, Jr.
        Committee Members

50th Graduation Reunion from Grambling State University, 1999

Commencement Exercises

TEXAS SOUTHERN UNIVERSITY

SUNDAY AFTERNOON, AUGUST TWENTY-EIGHTH

NINETEEN HUNDRED AND SIXTY

FIVE O'CLOCK

UNIVERSITY AUDITORIUM

HOUSTON, TEXAS

Epilogue

Speech delivered by Cynara Robinson at the funeral of
Annie Wiliams Adams, on December 2, 2006.

Good Afternoon!

It is an honor for me to be here paying tribute to my grandmother. Words cannot express my undying admiration for her.

Annie Williams Adams lived a life solid and true. She was a phenomenal example of an African American woman who was strong, educated, kind, good-hearted, and grounded in traditional values.

Growing up in New Orleans, although far from Mansfield, I remember always getting excited about coming to Mansfield. Those were fun trips as a kid. I remember always looking forward to the biscuits grandmother never failed to make for us every morning when we were staying with her. To this day, those are undoubtedly the best home-cooked biscuits I have ever tasted.

My admiration for her is endless. I admire how she achieved a bachelor's and a master's degree at a time when opportunities were extremely limited for black people; and she accomplished this as a black woman. I also admire how she did this, raised two daughters, advanced in her career as an educator, and remained a devoted wife.

And speaking of being a wife, I once spoke with her about how she met my grandfather. She told me the story of how they met at the train station in Mansfield one rainy day when she was coming back from Pleasant Hill, and grandfather came up to her and asked if she needed help with her luggage and she said "yes," and so began a relationship that became a long-lasting marriage.

My admiration for my grandmother was further manifested in my desire to use her experiences as a teacher for my own master's degree paper I wrote on the work of black women teachers in rural areas of pre-1950's Louisiana. In those interviews with her she spoke on some of her experiences teaching under Jim Crow conditions of that time. And I asked her about what it was like and how she made it work successfully with the limited resources to do her job, and one of her responses was, "We had some rough times. We had to take the things we could get and do the best we could to make things work."

And in my view of her life, she did just that. She used what she had and made it work. This is something I will always remember, admire, and love about her, her strong will.

Jean Adams Dickerson

Jean Adams Dickerson is a retired educator and is the older daughter of Annie. She and her younger sister, Cummie Adams Robinson, a retired educator, were privileged to be raised by this dedicated educator where most lessons learned were from teachable moments.

Jean's education career spanned forty-two years in school systems in Louisiana, California, Maryland and Texas. In those systems she served as teacher, counselor, administrator, and teacher certification specialist. At the university graduate level, she taught counseling and guidance. Her most coveted position was her work as a school counselor for twenty-one years serving elementary, middle, and high school students.

Jean has worked in teacher certification, selecting and training teachers to meet certification requirements.

Jean holds undergraduate and graduate degrees from Southern University, Baton Rouge, Louisiana; Northwestern State University, Natchitoches, Louisiana; and, California Lutheran University, Thousand Oaks, California.

For leisure, she enjoys travel and plays piano, golf, and tennis.

She is a member of Alpha Kappa Alpha Sorority, Incorporated.